WITHOUT

P O E T R Y   B Y
D O N A L D   H A L L

Exiles and Marriages (1955)

The Dark Houses (1958)

A Roof of Tiger Lilies (1964)

The Alligator Bride (1969)

The Yellow Room (1971)

The Town of Hill (1975)

Kicking the Leaves (1978)

The Happy Man (1986)

The One Day (1988)

Old and New Poems (1990)

The Museum of Clear Ideas (1993)

The Old Life (1996)

A Mariner Book

HOUGHTON MIFFLIN COMPANY   BOSTON   NEW YORK

Donald Hall

W I T H O U T

P O E M S

First Mariner Books edition 1999

For information about permission to reproduce selections from
this book, write to Permissions, Houghton Mifflin Company,
215 Park Avenue South, New York, New York 10003.

Design by Anne Chalmers
Type is Linotype Hell Fairfield

Printed in the United States of America

QUM 10 9 8 7 6 5 4 3 2 1

Library of Congress Cataloging-in-Publication Data
and permissions on page 84.

Page 9: *Timor mortis conturbat me.*
From William Dunbar's "Lament for the Makers":
The fear of death confounds me.

IN MEMORIAM

JANE KENYON

1947–1995

CONTENTS

WITHOUT

HER LONG ILLNESS

Daybreak until nightfall,
he sat by his wife at the hospital
        while chemotherapy dripped
through the catheter into her heart.
        He drank coffee and read
the *Globe*. He paced; he worked
        on poems; he rubbed her back
and read aloud. Overcome with dread,
        they wept and affirmed
their love for each other, witlessly,
        over and over again.
When it snowed one morning Jane gazed
        at the darkness blurred
with flakes. They pushed the IV pump
        which she called Igor
slowly past the nurses' pods, as far
        as the outside door
so that she could smell the snowy air.

"A BEARD FOR A BLUE PANTRY"

In Alice Mattison's dream
I have written a new poem I call
"A Beard for a Blue Pantry."

My wife who is her dear friend
has leukemia. I sit by Jane's bed
as white cells proliferate

and petechiae bloom on her skin.
The summer after we married
I grew a black beard, and Jane

wrote a poem on the airplane
flying home from California:
"The First Eight Days of the Beard."

A dozen years later I shaved
when the beard turned as white
as King Arthur Flour

in the pantry where Bluebeard
the cat birdwatched out the window
from his perch on the breadbox.

In those deliberate days,
Jane made bread so honest
it once went blue in the pantry

overnight in a heat wave.
Each morning we worked together
apart, I in my downstairs study

and Jane at her rolltop desk
above the kitchen, making poems
until dew dried and she mulched

her roses; or she filled the feeder
with sunflower seed, or walked the dog
in snow, or answered Alice's letter,

or washed her abundant hair
which is gone now, like Bluebeard
who sickened and dwindled away.

Home a week. He looked
back in the calendar. February
was slashed kitty-corner
with Jane's shaky large block capitals
staggering eight letters
out: L E U K E M I A

"This morning Gussie
woke me up. I let him out, fed Ada,
    took Gus back in again,
and fed him. Then I went to the bathroom
    to pee, and saw myself
in the mirror. I had forgotten
    the bald woman with
leukemia who stared back at me."

SONG FOR LUCY

She died quickly at ninety,
when Jane had been sick
for two months only.
I remember my mother
skinny in her early thirties,

when I was seven and eight.
Unable to sleep
or unwilling, I would call
— waiting in the dark
to hear her footsteps —

and she would climb the stairs
to sing in my ear
with her narrow voice,
without a tune, but with
love-sounds like milk:

"Just a song at twilight,"
"Keep the home fires
burning," "There's a long, long
trail a-winding, into
the land of my dreams."

She nursed so well, I loved
being sick. Freud said
a man thrives his whole life
if he received as a child
"his mother's entire devotion."

I remember her at forty
— nervous, wearing lipstick —
drinking Scotch and vomiting
to drink more Scotch,
behaving as good companion

to my depressed father. Both
were feckless at being drunks
and abandoned the project
when he hemorrhaged at forty-two.
They were content together

the decade before he died
as she rubbed his shaking
head. She wasn't feeble
until eighty when a congestive
heart took her force away.

She responded not with fury
but by measuring affection
and declaring its rapture.
How fervent her soul became,
lucid through her blue eyes:

Love was her enterprise.
She died before I could reach her.
Jane felt strong that day
as we emptied Lucy's room,
and ate a leftover cookie.

This time they put Jane
in the East Wing — no room in the Bubble —
    but he kept forgetting.
One afternoon, absent-mindedly
    approaching Pod 4's glassed-in
comfort and safety, he saw someone
    hurl through the heavy door
howling, erupting tears, staggering,
    followed by a nurse
who touched her and led her away.
    When he returned to Jane,
he did not tell her what he had seen.
    Later an orderly told them
there was a bed for her in the Bubble.

Alone together a moment
on the twenty-second anniversary
        of their wedding,
he clasped her as she stood
        at the sink, pressing
into her backside, rubbing his cheek
        against the stubble
of her skull. He gave her a ring
        of pink tourmaline
with nine small diamonds around it.
        She put it on her finger
and immediately named it Please Don't Die.
        They kissed and Jane
whispered, "Timor mortis conturbat me."

THE PORCELAIN COUPLE

When Jane felt well enough for me to leave her
a whole day, I drove south by the river
to empty my mother's house in Connecticut.
I hurried from room to room, cellar to attic,
looking into a crammed storeroom, then turning
to discover a chest with five full drawers.
I labeled for shipping sofas and chairs,
bedroom sets, and tables; I wrapped figurines
and fancy teacups in paper, preserving
things she had cherished — and in late years dreaded
might go for a nickel at a sale on the lawn.
Everywhere I saw shelves and tabletops
covered with glass animals and music boxes.
In closets, decades of finery hung in dead air.
I swept ashtrays and blouses into plastic sacks,
and the green-gold dress she wore to Bermuda.
At the last moment I discovered and saved
a cut-glass tumbler, stained red at the top,
Lucy 1905 scripted on the stain. In the garage
I piled bags for the dump, then drove four hours
north with my hands tight on the steering wheel,
drank a beer looking through the day's mail,
and pitched into bed with Jane who slept fitfully.
When I woke, I rose as if from a drunken sleep
after looting a city and burning its temples.
All day, while I ate lunch or counted out pills,
I noticed the objects of our twenty years:
a blue vase, a candelabrum Jane carried on her lap
from the Baja, and the small porcelain box
from France I found under the tree one Christmas
where a couple in relief stretch out asleep,
like a catafalque, on the pastel double bed
of the box's top, both wearing pretty nightcaps.

When they courted, Jane's hair
was short and straight, easy to care for.
        Later she grew it long,
below her shoulders, and wrote poems
        from the cave behind it.
In New Hampshire, as she grew older,
        her hair flourished — thick,
curled, sensuous, massed with its white
        streak around her exaggerated
features. He slipped through its waterfall
        to the mossy darkness
behind its flowing. When she was forty
        she came into her beauty
as into a fortune — eyes, cheekbones, nose,
        and thickwater hair.
                                Today,
she looked at her bald head and at
        her face swollen
with prednisone: "I am Telly Savalas."

When he roiled in Recovery
after the surgeon cut out half his liver
      two years earlier,
Jane pushed the morphine bolus.
      She brought him home,
a breathing sarcophagus, then rubbed his body
      back to life with her hands.
Now, rocking on the bed in their horror,
      they wept and held on
against the proliferation of her blasts,
      murmuring together
of what adhered them. This ardent
      merging recollected
old passionate connections at two
      in the afternoon:
brief, breathless, ecstatic, then calm.

He hovered beside Jane's bed,
solicitous: "What can I *do?*"
    It must have been unbearable
while she suffered her private hurts
    to see his worried face
looming above her, always anxious to *do*
    something when there was
exactly nothing to do. Inside him,
    some four-year-old
understood that if he was good — thoughtful,
    considerate, beyond
reproach, *perfect* — she would not leave him.

Why were they not
contented, four months ago, because
         Jane did not have
leukemia? A year hence, would he question
         why he was not contented
now? Therefore he was contented.

Following the protocol
for ALL, now the doctors began
         the Fourth Intensification —
two weeks of infusions, shots, and nausea.
         Already, since Ara-C,
Jane used a walker, slept fourteen hours,
         and believed that they lived
on the Newport Road of her childhood.
         This morning she asked where
Bluebeard was, their cat who died long ago.

THE SHIP POUNDING

Each morning I made my way
among gangways, elevators,
and nurses' pods to Jane's room
to interrogate the grave helpers
who tended her through the night
while the ship's massive engines
kept its propellers turning.
Week after week, I sat by her bed
with black coffee and the *Globe*.
The passengers on this voyage
wore masks or cannulae
or dangled devices that dripped
chemicals into their wrists.
I believed that the ship
traveled to a harbor
of breakfast, work, and love.
I wrote: "When the infusions
are infused entirely, bone
marrow restored and lymphoblasts
remitted, I will take my wife,
bald as Michael Jordan,
back to our dog and day." Today,
months later at home, these
words turned up on my desk
as I listened in case Jane called
for help, or spoke in delirium,
ready to make the agitated
drive to Emergency again
for readmission to the huge

vessel that heaves water month
after month, without leaving
port, without moving a knot,
without arrival or destination,
its great engines pounding.

When their minister,
Alice Ling, brought communion to the house
    or the hospital bed,
or when they held hands as Alice prayed,
    grace was evident
but not the comfort of mercy or reprieve.
    The embodied figure
on the cross still twisted under the sun.

AIR SHATTERS IN THE
CAR'S SMALL ROOM

Distracting myself
on the recliner between
Jane's hospital bed
and window, in this blue
room where we endure,
I set syllables
into prosy lines.
William Butler Yeats
denounced with passion
"the poetry of
passive suffering."
Friends and strangers
write letters speaking
of courage or strength.
What else could we do
except what we do?
Should we weep lying
flat? We do. Sometimes,
driving the Honda
with its windows closed
in beginning autumn
from the low motel
to Jane's bed, I scream
and keep on screaming.

They flew all day across
the country to the hospital for hard cases.
    The night before Jane
entered isolation in Seattle for chemo,
    TBI, and a stranger's
bone marrow — for life or death — they slept
    together, as they understood,
maybe for the last time. His body
    curved into Jane's,
his knees tucked to the backs of her knees;
    he pressed her warm soft thighs,
back, waist, and rump, making the spoons,
    and the spoons clattered
with a sound like the end man's bones.

As they killed her bone
marrow again, she lay on a gurney
alone in a leaden
room between machines that resembled
pot-bellied stoves
which spewed out Total Body Irradiation
for eleven half-hour
sessions measured over four days.
It was as if she capped
the Chernobyl pile with her body.

The courier brought
bone marrow in an insulated bottle
        from the donor, a nameless
thirty-nine-year-old female who
        sent along words
"To the Recipient." Jane's
        "For the Donor" flew back
somewhere, where a stranger lay flat
        with an anesthetic
hangover and pelvic bones that ached —
        and with disinterested
love, which is the greatest of these.

        Jane lay silent on her back
as pink liquid leached through a tube
        from a six-inch-square
plastic envelope. It was Day Zero.

By Day Eleven, mucositis
from the burn of Total Body Irradiation
        frayed her mouth apart
cell by cell, peeling her lips and tongue.

        To enter her antibiotic
cube, it took him fifteen minutes
        to suit up, wearing a wide
paper hat, yellow mask, long white
        booties like a Dallas
Cowgirl, blue paper surgical gown,
        and sterile latex gloves.
Jane said he looked like a huge condom.

He woke at five, brewed
coffee, swallowed pills, injected insulin,
shaved, ate breakfast, packed
the tote with Jane's sweats he washed
at night, filled the thermos,
and left the apartment on Spring Street
to walk a block and a half
to the hospital's bone marrow floor.
Waiting for the light
to cross the avenue, briefly he imagined
throwing himself in front
of that bus. He knew he wouldn't.

Discharged at last,
she returned to sleep with him again
in the flat jerry-built
for bald tenants and their caregivers.
He counted out meds
and programmed pumps to deliver
hydration, TPN,
and ganciclovir. He needed to learn
from Maggie Fisher the nurse
how to assemble the tubing, to insert
narrow ends into
wide ones. "From long experience," Maggie
told him, "I have learned
to distinguish 'male' from 'female.'"

As Dr. McDonald plunged
the tube down her throat, her body thrashed
        on the table. When she
struggled to rise, the doctor's voice cajoled,
        "Jane, Jane," until
blood-oxygen numbers dropped toward zero
        and her face went blue.
The young nurse slipped oxygen into Jane's
        nostrils and punched
a square button. Eight doctors burst
        into the room, someone
pounded Jane's chest, Dr. McDonald
        gave orders like
a submarine captain among depth charges,
        the nurse fixed
a nebulizer over Jane's mouth and nose —
        and she breathed.
                        Meanwhile,
understanding that his wife might be dying
        before his eyes, he stood still,
careful to keep out of everyone's way.

While Jane suffered
to survive, her mother lay dying
    three thousand miles away.
Jane telephoned each day when she could
    to talk with Polly
or her nurses as Polly's radiation
    accomplished only
dehydration, burning skin, and nausea.
    "It's been a pretty
good day; I ate soup and apple juice."
    "She seems comfortable."
"Her eyes are rolling back." "Soon."

Jane wasn't certain
where she was, the month or the year, or who
was President. An ambulance
took her from the clinic two blocks
back to the hospital.
Her thinking returned slowly. With it came
depression, the desire
to die with her mother, and loathing
for the view of Seattle
from an eleventh-floor window
that in the autumn
had given her pleasure: "I hate this city."
She spoke to him in anger:
"I wish you could feel what I feel!"

Her one rebuke became
his nightmare: At Eagle Pond, Jane
sprayed his body with acid
from a booby trap. He was dying.
He followed her in his rage
to Connecticut and his mother's house.
Just before he woke, he saw
Jane crouched in terror at the bottom
of the cellar stairs while he
crept down, his hands clutched to choke her.

At four every afternoon
Jane started to fret or panic.
    On a Monday he lay
on the sofa with mild vertigo,
    but Jane was sure
it was a heart attack or embolism,
    no matter what he said.
Paramedics from an ambulance took
    his EKG for Jane's sake.
A day later, Jane couldn't stand or walk.
    Back in the hospital
she believed that she had never been sick
    and would be discovered,
that Blue Cross and the hospital would sue
    and take away their house.
It did not matter what he told her,
    but Haldol and Klonopin
mattered. For two hours she dozed; when
    she woke, she no longer
insisted, "I am a wicked person."

A volunteer drove them
to baggage, wheelchair, and USAir
        frequent traveler
first-class seats. In Pittsburgh a cart
        delivered them to the gate
for Manchester, New Hampshire, where
        the children held up posters
and placards that their children had crayoned.
        They waved and leapt
as Jane walked without help down the ramp
        to the wheelchair,
to the heated car, to the hour's ride home.

All through the house
they found relics of Polly's absence
        — a woolly pink beret,
her magazines of sewing and fashion,
        garments she made,
and *The Golden Bowl* she had interrupted,
        their November postcard
keeping a place, halfway through.

BLUES FOR POLLY

Jane's bookcase and chest of drawers
carried the family pictures:
slim Reuel and Polly posing
on the porch with the children
in 1952, ordinary-seeming
people in an improvised house
full of art and no money: books,
paintings, fabrics, pottery.
As a child Jane went to sleep
in her bedroom above the hi-fi
that played Haydn, Fats Waller,
Ives, and Mozart.

      The whole family
made puns at the dinner table,
argued politics, and neglected
to mention their grievances
with one another — although rage
might steam like spaghetti *al olio*.
Art was dependable, something
to live for.

    At five-thirty
on a Sunday morning in October
under the yellow porch light
we said goodbye to Polly. We hugged
weeping, and our friend loaded us
into his Jeep for the airport
and maybe continuing life.
Polly grew small behind us,
wrapped in her long housecoat
and waving farewell, with Gus

flopped down dejected
beside her.

A month after Polly
died and we flew back home,
in her room we discovered a glossy
photograph:

Polly was singing
with a band in a Chicago nightclub —
eighteen years old, pretty,
the minister's ambitious daughter
just out of high school, excitement
and terror enlarging her eyes
as she made her sorrowful noise
to the Lord in a smoky room
of gamblers, gangsters, and girls.
She sang blue: soulful, erotic,
skeptical, knowing everything
turns out bad in the end.

At home each day budged
forward — more calories (Ensure Plus,
    cream cheese and jelly,
macaroni and cheese), more exercise
    (two hundred yards'
joyous walking with Gus), and, tentatively,
    the first phrases
dictated toward what might be a poem.

They hired a movie each
afternoon — Jane could read a short story
        for half an hour — and at bedtime
he helped her take off her sweatpants
        and pull on the blue-striped
flannel nightgown Caroline gave her.
        It was reasonable
to expect that in ten or twelve months
        she would be herself.
She would dress and eat her breakfast.
        She would drive her Saab
to shop for groceries.
                        He felt shame
        to understand he would miss
the months of sickness and taking care.

LAST DAYS

"It was reasonable
to expect." So he wrote. The next day,
in a consultation room,
Jane's hematologist Letha Mills sat down,
stiff, her assistant
standing with her back to the door.
"I have terrible news,"
Letha told them. "The leukemia is back.
There's nothing to do."
The four of them wept. He asked how long,
why did it happen now?
Jane asked only: "Can I die at home?"

Home that afternoon,
they threw her medicines into the trash.
Jane vomited. He wailed
while she remained dry-eyed — silent,
trying to let go. At night
he picked up the telephone to make
calls that brought
a child or a friend into the horror.

The next morning,
they worked choosing among her poems
    for *Otherwise*, picked
hymns for her funeral, and supplied each
    other words as they wrote
and revised her obituary. The day after,
    with more work to do
on her book, he saw how weak she felt,
    and said maybe not now; tomorrow?
Jane shook her head: "Now," she said.
    "We have to finish it now."
Later, as she slid exhausted into sleep,
    she said, "Wasn't that fun?
To work together? Wasn't that fun?"

He asked her, "What clothes
should we dress you in, when we bury you?"
        "I hadn't thought," she said.
"I wondered about the white salwar
        kameez," he said —
her favorite Indian silk they bought
        in Pondicherry a year
and a half before, which she wore for best
        or prettiest afterward.
She smiled. "Yes. Excellent," she said.
        He didn't tell her
that a year earlier, dreaming awake,
        he had seen her
in the coffin in her white salwar kameez.

Still, he couldn't stop
planning. That night he broke out with,
        "When Gus dies I'll
have him cremated and scatter his ashes
        on your grave!" She laughed
and her big eyes quickened and she nodded:
        "It will be good
for the daffodils." She lay pallid back
        on the flowered pillow:
"Perkins, how do you *think* of these things?"

They talked about their
adventures — driving through England
    when they first married,
and excursions to China and India.
    Also they remembered
ordinary days — pond summers, working
    on poems together,
walking the dog, reading Chekhov
    aloud. When he praised
thousands of afternoon assignations
    that carried them into
bliss and repose on this painted bed,
    Jane burst into tears
and cried, "No more fucking. No more fucking!"

Incontinent three nights
before she died, Jane needed lifting
    onto the commode.
He wiped her and helped her back into bed.
    At five he fed the dog
and returned to find her across the room,
    sitting in a straight chair.
When she couldn't stand, how could she walk?
    He feared she would fall
and called for an ambulance to the hospital,
    but when he told Jane,
her mouth twisted down and tears started.
    "Do we have to?" He canceled.
Jane said, "Perkins, be with me when I die."

"Dying is simple," she said.
"What's worst is . . . *the separation*."
      When she no longer spoke,
they lay alone together, touching,
      and she fixed on him
her beautiful enormous round brown eyes,
      shining, unblinking,
and passionate with love and dread.

One by one they came,
the oldest and dearest, to say goodbye
        to this friend of the heart.
At first she said their names, wept, and touched;
        then she smiled; then
turned one mouth-corner up. On the last day
        she stared silent goodbyes
with her hands curled and her eyes stuck open.

Leaving his place beside her,
where her eyes stared, he told her,
    "I'll put these letters
in the box." She had not spoken
    for three hours, and now Jane said
her last words: "O.K."

                    At eight that night,
    her eyes open as they stayed
until she died, brain-stem breathing
    started, he bent to kiss
her pale cool lips again, and felt them
    one last time gather
and purse and peck to kiss him back.

In the last hours, she kept
her forearms raised with pale fingers clenched
        at cheek level, like
the goddess figurine over the bathroom sink.
        Sometimes her right fist flicked
or spasmed toward her face. For twelve hours
        until she died, he kept
scratching Jane Kenyon's big bony nose.
        A sharp, almost sweet
smell began to rise from her open mouth.
        He watched her chest go still.
With his thumb he closed her round brown eyes.

WITHOUT

we lived in a small island stone nation
without color under gray clouds and wind
distant the unlimited ocean acute
lymphoblastic leukemia without seagulls
or palm trees without vegetation
or animal life only barnacles and lead
colored moss that darkened when months did

hours days weeks months weeks days hours
the year endured without punctuation
february without ice winter sleet
snow melted recovered but nothing
without thaw although cold streams hurtled
no snowdrop or crocus rose no yellow
no red leaves of maple without october

no spring no summer no autumn no winter
no rain no peony thunder no woodthrush
the book was a thousand pages without commas
without mice oak leaves windstorms
no castles no plazas no flags no parrots
without carnival or the procession of relics
intolerable without brackets or colons

silence without color sound without smell
without apples without pork to rupture gnash
unpunctuated without churches uninterrupted
no orioles ginger noses no opera no
without fingers daffodils cheekbones
the body was a nation a tribe dug into stone
assaulted white blood broken to shards

provinces invaded bombed shot shelled
artillery sniper fire helicopter gunship
grenade burning murder landmine starvation
the ceasefire lasted forty-eight hours
then a shell exploded in a market
pain vomit neuropathy morphine nightmare
confusion the rack terror the vise

vincristine ara-c cytoxan vp-16
loss of memory loss of language losses
pneumocystis carinii pneumonia bactrim
foamless unmitigated sea without sea
delirium whipmarks of petechiae
multiple blisters of herpes zoster
and how are you doing today I am doing

one afternoon say the sun came out
moss took on greenishness leaves fell
the market opened a loaf of bread a sparrow
a bony dog wandered back sniffing a lath
it might be possible to take up a pencil
unwritten stanzas taken up and touched
beautiful terrible sentences unuttered

the sea unrelenting wave gray the sea
flotsam without islands broken crates
block after block the same house the mall
no cathedral no hobo jungle the same women
and men they longed to drink hayfields no
without dog or semicolon or village square
without monkey or lily without garlic

THE GALLERY

Back home from the grave,
behind my desk I made
a gallery of Janes:
at twenty-four, with long
straight hair sitting
beside me in my Pittsburgh
Pirate suit; standing
recessive in shadow
wearing her nearsighted
glasses, Kearsarge behind us;
stretched out glamorous
in her bathing suit
at Key West; foxy
and beautiful at forty-five;
embracing me last year;
front page of the Sunday
Concord Monitor
in color with headline:
POET JANE KENYON DIES
AT HER HOME IN WILMOT.

LETTER WITH NO ADDRESS

Your daffodils rose up
and collapsed in their yellow
bodies on the hillside
garden above the bricks
you laid out in sand, squatting
with pants pegged and face
masked like a beekeeper's
against the black flies.
Buttercups circle the planks
of the old wellhead
this May while your silken
gardener's body withers or moulds
in the Proctor graveyard.
I drive and talk to you crying
and come back to this house
to talk to your photographs.

There's news to tell you:
Maggie Fisher's pregnant.
I carried myself like an egg
at Abigail's birthday party
a week after you died,
as three-year-olds bounced
uproarious on a mattress.
Joyce and I met for lunch
at the mall and strolled weepily
through Sears and B. Dalton.

Today it's four weeks
since you lay on our painted bed
and I closed your eyes.
Yesterday I cut irises to set

in a pitcher on your grave;
today I brought a carafe
to fill it with fresh water.
I remember bone pain,
vomiting, delirium. I remember
pond afternoons.

                    My routine
is established: coffee;
the *Globe*; breakfast;
writing you this letter
at my desk. When I go to bed
to sleep after baseball,
Gus follows me into the bedroom
as he used to follow us.
Most of the time he flops
down in the parlor
with his head on his paws.

Once a week I drive to Tilton
to see Dick and Nan.
Nan doesn't understand much
but she knows you're dead;
I feel her fretting. The tune
of Dick and me talking
seems to console her.

                    You know now
whether the soul survives death.
Or you don't. When you were dying
you said you didn't fear
punishment. We never dared
to speak of Paradise.

At five A.M., when I walk outside,
mist lies thick on hayfields.
By eight the air is clear,
cool, sunny with the pale yellow
light of mid-May. Kearsarge
rises huge and distinct,
each birch and balsam visible.
To the west the waters
of Eagle Pond waver
and flash through popples just
leafing out.

        Always the weather,
writing its book of the world,
returns you to me.
Ordinary days were best,
when we worked over poems
in our separate rooms.
I remember watching you gaze
out the January window
into the garden of snow
and ice, your face rapt
as you imagined burgundy lilies.

Your presence in this house
is almost as enormous
and painful as your absence.
Driving home from Tilton,
I remember how you cherished
that vista with its center
the red door of a farmhouse
against green fields.

Are you past pity?
If you have consciousness now,
if something I can call
"you" has something
like "consciousness," I doubt
you remember the last days.
I play them over and over:
I lift your wasted body
onto the commode, your arms
looped around my neck, aiming
your bony bottom so that
it will not bruise on a rail.
Faintly you repeat,
"Momma, Momma."

     You lay
astonishing in the long box
while Alice Ling prayed
and sang "Amazing Grace"
a cappella.

    Three times today
I drove to your grave.
Sometimes, coming back home
to our circular driveway,
I imagine you've returned
before me, bags of groceries upright
in the back of the Saab,
its trunk lid delicately raised
as if proposing an encounter,
dog-fashion, with the Honda.

INDEPENDENCE DAY LETTER

Five A.M., the Fourth of July.
I walk by Eagle Pond with the dog,
wearing my leather coat
against the clear early chill,
looking at water lilies that clutch
cool yellow fists together,
as I undertake another day
twelve weeks after the Tuesday
we learned that you would die.

This afternoon I'll pay bills
and write a friend about her book
and watch Red Sox baseball.
I'll walk Gussie again.
I'll microwave some Stouffer's.
A woman will drive from Bristol
to examine your mother's Ford
parked beside your Saab
in the dead women's used car lot.

Tonight the Andover fireworks
will have to go on without me
as I go to bed early, reading
The Man Without Qualities
with insufficient attention
because I keep watching you die.
Tomorrow I will wake at five
to the tenth Wednesday
after the Wednesday we buried you.

Sitting in a swivel chair,
wearing slacks, blazer, and tie
among distinguished patrons
and administrators
of the arts, I let my eyes shut
for the flash of sleep
required to get by. "Proactive"
had become the leitmotif
of discourse. When I woke,
I wrote these lines on a pad,
hoping I appeared to be taking
a dutiful note, as in, "Always
remember: *Remain proactive.*"

If a councilor glanced at me,
I looked downward quickly.
I was there; I was elsewhere,
in that room I never leave
where I sit beside you listening
to your altered breathing,
three quick inhalations
and a pause. I keep my body
before your large wide-open eyes
that do not blink or waver,
in case they might finally see
— sitting beside you, attentive —
the one who will close them.

MIDSUMMER LETTER

The polished black granite
cemented over your head
reflects the full moon of August
four months from the day
your chest went still.
For you, the gloom of August
was annual; you watched
the red leaves on Huldah's maple
burn down your summer's day.

Kate MacKay had me to supper
in Grafton, to read your poems
to our Hitchcock nurses.
Mary hooted when I read "The Shirt."
Walking to the car, I was happy
under the summer night, harsh
with stars.

        Nan died Wednesday.
Remember, when we visited her,
how you painted her nails pink
and she spread her fingers out,
unable to speak but grateful.
Alone after fifty-five years,
Dick is heartsick.

        We scattered
your mother's ashes in Eagle Pond
at the same spot where, a dozen
years ago, we watched your father's
float and sink. When your brother

cast Polly's into a scud of wind,
they opened in a glinting swarm
and plunged into water.

                                    I flew
to Washington for the Council.
It was desolate to return
through the Manchester airport
where we left the plane in triumph
last February. Remember,
after we drove to the farm,
how Gus sniffed you carefully,
as if you might be an impostor,
and when you checked out,
sang half an hour
beside you, his voice trilling
like a countertenor's.

I can't play your CDs or tapes.
In Symphony Hall I sat beside you,
witnessing as your spirit
hovered like a hummingbird.
Every day I look at the words
cut into stone, which you wrote
when I was supposed to die:

I BELIEVE IN THE MIRACLES OF ART BUT WHAT
PRODIGY WILL KEEP YOU SAFE BESIDE ME

Most days I wake at five-thirty
to work on these poems.

Then I turn to the taxes, read mail
and answer it — one thing
after another. But last week,
being photographed, I sat
still and speechless for ninety minutes
posing by daylilies and barns
and my idle mind entered
the coffin, where even the white
of your salwar kameez
was absolute blackness. My mind
made a jingle, rhyming
"ants" with "lips."

            Philippa brought
the children from Concord
to wade in Eagle Pond. Allison
showed me a wild strawberry plant.
Abigail snatched at minnows
and laughed. For an hour
I watched them play, my tall grave
daughter beside me.

            The hour
we lived in, two decades
by the pond, has transformed
into a single unstoppable day,
gray in the dwelling-place
of absence. Tonight I sat
in nighttime silence by the open
window and heard the peepers' soprano
and the bass bullfrogs'

percussion repeating the August
nocturne we went to bed by.
I'll never read Henry James
aloud to you again. We'll never laugh
and grunt again as your face
turns from apparent agony
to repose, and you tell me
it registered 7.2
on the Richter scale.

               Last night
before sleep I walked out
to look at the cold summer moon
as it rose over Ragged Mountain.
I slept six hours,
then woke in the dark morning
to see it huge in the west
as if this were any August.

LETTER IN AUTUMN

This first October of your death
I sit in my blue chair
looking out at late afternoon's
western light suffusing
its goldenrod yellow over
the barn's unpainted boards —
here where I sat each fall
watching you pull your summer's
garden up.

            Yesterday
I cleaned out your Saab
to sell it. The dozen tapes
I mailed to Caroline.
I collected hairpins and hair ties.
In the Hill's Balsam tin
where you kept silver for tolls
I found your collection
of slips from fortune cookies:
YOU ARE A FANTASTIC PERSON!
YOU ARE ONE OF THOSE PEOPLE
WHO GOES PLACES IN THEIR LIFE!

As I slept last night:
You leap from our compartment
in an underground railroad yard
and I follow; behind us the train
clatters and sways; I turn
and turn again to see you tugging
at a gold bugle welded
to a freight car; then you vanish
into the pitchy clanking dark.

Here I sit in my blue chair
not exactly watching Seattle
beat Denver in the Kingdome.
Last autumn above Pill Hill
we looked from the eleventh floor
down at Puget Sound,
at Seattle's skyline,
and at the Kingdome scaffolded
for repair. From your armature
of tubes, you asked, "Perkins,
am I going to live?"

                When you died
in April, baseball took up
its cadences again
under the indoor ballpark's
patched and recovered ceiling.
You would have admired
the Mariners, still hanging on
in October, like blue asters
surviving frost.

                Sometimes
when I start to cry,
I wave it off: "I just
did that." When Andrew
wearing a dark suit and necktie
telephones from his desk,
he cannot keep from crying.
When Philippa weeps,
Allison at seven announces,
"The river is flowing."

Gus no longer searches for you,
but when Alice or Joyce comes calling
he dances and sings. He brings us
one of your white slippers
from the bedroom.

                    I cannot discard
your jeans or lotions or T-shirts.
I cannot disturb your tumbles
of scarves and floppy hats.
Lost unfinished things remain
on your desk, in your purse
or Shaker basket. Under a cushion
I discover your silver thimble.
Today when the telephone rang
I thought it was you.

At night when I go to bed
Gus drowses on the floor beside me.
I sleep where we lived and died
in the painted Victorian bed
under the tiny lights
you strung on the headboard
when you brought me home
from the hospital four years ago.
The lights still burned last April
early on a Saturday morning
while you died.

                    At your grave
I find tribute: chrysanthemums,
cosmos, a pumpkin, and a poem

by a woman who "never knew you"
who asks, "Can you hear me Jane?"
There is an apple and a heart-
shaped pebble.

        Looking south
from your stone, I gaze at the file
of eight enormous sugar maples
that rage and flare in dark noon,
the air grainy with mist
like the rain of Seattle's winter.
The trees go on burning
without ravage of loss or disorder.
I wish you were that birch
rising from the clump behind you,
and I the gray oak alongside.

LETTER AT CHRISTMAS

The big wooden clock you gave me
our first Christmas together
stopped in September.
The Bristol Watch Maker
kept it six weeks. Now it speeds
sixty-five minutes to the hour, as if
it wants to be done with the day.

When I try talking with strangers
I want to run out of the room
into the woods with turkeys and foxes.
I want to talk only
about words we spoke back and forth
when we knew you would die.
I want never to joke or argue
or chatter again. I want never
to think or feel.

                    Maggie Fisher
mailed pictures of the baby.
On Thanksgiving I brought Dick
from Tilton to Andrew's for dinner.
Peter grinned; we hugged Ariana
and conversed with Emily.
For three hours we played,
teased, laughed together.
Suddenly I had to drive home.

Yesterday I caught sight of you
in the Kearsarge Mini-Mart.

The first snow fell seven months
from the day you died.
We used to gaze at the early snow
where it heaped like sugar
or salt on boulders, barn roofs,
fence posts, and gravestones.
No one plows Cemetery Road;
I will miss visiting you
when snow is deep.

     In Advent
for twenty years you opened
the calendar's daily window;
you fixed candles in a wreath
for church; you read the Gospels
over again each year:
The Child would be born again.

Most years we woke up by six
to empty our stockings.
You gave me Post-Its, paperclips,
shortbread, #1 pencils,
and blank books. I gave you
felt pens, paperclips, chocolate,
and something libidinous
in the toe.

    I remember
only one miserable Christmas.
You were so depressed
that the spidery lace of a shawl
and a terra-cotta Etruscan woman

only left you feeling
worthless, stupid, and ugly.
Melancholy still thickens
its filaments over the presents
I gave you that morning.

Even last December
when our petrochemical three-foot
balsam stood on a glass
tabletop in that gimcrack Seattle
apartment, you strung it
with tiny lights, interrupting
your task to vomit. Bald
as Brancusi's egg, with limbs
as thin as a Giacometti strider,
you sat diminished
in a soft chair, among pumps
and bags. I programmed
the Provider for twelve hours
of hyperalimentation. Wearing
plastic gloves, I set up
the Bard-Harvard infusion
device to deliver ganciclovir.

Before your November transplant,
you had ordered me
loafers from L. L. Bean.
From another catalog you bought
flowery green-and-white sheets.
I gave you a black MoMA
briefcase and cashmere sweats
from Neiman-Marcus.

You preened, rubbing the softness
against your face.

                    Your feast
last year was applesauce
for pills, Ensure Plus,
and an inch square of bread
and jelly. I read you
from Luke's Gospel, then John's;
and then we fell silent
as the Child was born —
adored, clung to, irreparable.

                    *

This first Advent alone
I feed the small birds of snow
black-oil sunflower seed
as you used to do. Every day
I stand trembling with joy
to watch them: Fat mourning doves
compete with red squirrels
for spill from rampaging nuthatches
with rusty breasts
and black-and-white face masks.

This year late autumn darkness
punishes me as it used
to punish you. For decades,
when December night closed in
midafternoon and you suffered,
I hunched by the reddening

Glenwood, finding the darkness
a comfort. Feeding your birds
consoles me now. If you
were writing this letter,
what would you turn to now?
Maybe you'd look at the mouse
that Ada offers.

                    This year
there's no tree for Gus to sniff
and Ada to leap at, dislodging
an ornament from your childhood.
I toss the dead mouse outside
on Christmas afternoon
and wash my hands at the sink
as I look at Mount Kearsarge
through the kitchen window
where you stood to watch the birds.
Often I came up behind you
and pushed against your bottom.
This year, home from unwrapping
presents with grandchildren
and children, sick with longing,
I press my penis
into zinc and butcherblock.

LETTER IN THE NEW YEAR

New Year's Eve I baby-sat
the girls in Concord, napping
on the sofa. In Seattle
last year we slept through
as usual, except that your sugar
went crazy from prednisone.
I pricked your finger
every four hours all night
and shot insulin.

        The year
of your death was not usual
and this new year is offensive
because it will not contain you.

For six months Gus flung himself
down in the parlor all day,
sighing enormous sighs.
Now he lies beside me
where I sit in my blue chair
eating bagels in the morning,
watching basketball by night,
or beside our black-and-gold bed
where I read and sleep.
Ada curls on my other side.
I'm what they've got;
they know it.

        Stepping outside,
I check the weather to tell you:
The sun is invisible, still
ascending behind Ragged,

but west of the pond its rays
pass overhead to light
the snow on Eagle's Nest.
The moon blanches in a clear sky,
with one cloud scudding
to the south over Kearsarge,
which turns lavender at dawn.
Time for the desk again.
I tell Gus, "Poetryman
is suiting up!"

       The bulletin
this January is snow.
New Canada is a "One Lane Road"
along the old pasture's woodlot.
The hills collapse together
in whiteness squared out
by stone walls that contain
wavery birches and boulders
softened into breasts. White
yards and acres of snowfield
reflect the full moon,
and at noontime the sky
turns its deepest blue
of the year. I puff as Gussie
and I walk over packed snow
at zero, my heart quick
with joy in the visible world.

Do you remember our first
January at Eagle Pond,
the coldest in a century?

It dropped to thirty-eight below —
with no furnace, no storm
windows or insulation.
We sat reading or writing
in our two big chairs, either
side of the Glenwood,
and made love on the floor
with the stove open and roaring.
You were twenty-eight.
If someone had told us then
you would die in nineteen years,
would it have sounded
like almost enough time?

This month Philippa and her family
moved into a house they built
on wooded land in Bow.
Each girl has her own room.
I gave Abigail a bookcase
and Allison a grown-up oak desk.
As I read them storybooks
on the sofa, I thought of you
making clothespin dolls
with Allison, to put on a show;
you were supporting actress.

When you were dying, you fretted:
"What will become of Perkins?"
The children telephone
each morning. Sometimes our friends
visit and raise you up.

I meet Galway and Bobbie
in Norwich; Bobbie consoles me,
wearing your Christmas
cashmere sweats. Liam and Tree
bounce and exaggerate
the way we four did together.
When Alice took Amtrak
and Concord Trailways to visit
before Christmas, we watched
the Sunday school pageant.

Sometimes I weep for an hour
twisted in the fetal position
as you did in depression.
Hypochondriac, I fret over Gus
and decide he's got diabetes.
In daydream I spend afternoons
digging around your peonies
to feed them my grandfather's
fifty-year-old cow manure.
Next week maybe I'll menstruate.

I want to hear you laugh again,
your throaty whoop. Every day
I imagine you widowed
in this house of purposeful quiet.
You would have confided in Gus
and reproached Ada, lunched
with friends in New London,
climbed Kearsarge, wept,
written poems, and lain unmoving,

eyes open, in bed all morning.
You would have found
a lover, but not right away.
I want to fuck you
in Paradise. "The sexual
intercourse of angels," Yeats
in old age wrote his old
love, "is a conflagration
of the whole being."

POSTCARD: JANUARY 22ND

I grew heavy through summer and autumn
and now I bear your death. I feed her,
bathe her, rock her, and change her diapers.
She lifts her small skull, trembling
and tentative. She smiles, spits up, shits
in a toilet, learns to read and multiply.
I watch her grow, prosper, thrive.
She is the darling of her mother's old age.

MIDWINTER LETTER

I wanted this assaulting winter
to end before January ended.
But I want everything to end.
I lean forward from emptiness
eager for more emptiness:
the next thing! the next thing!

The thaw arrived as the front loader
departed: warm sun, slush, then
forty-eight hours of downpour.
Snowdrifts decomposed by the house.
Walker Brook tore ice blocks
loose with a clamor
that worried Gus as we walked
beside the filthy flesh
of old snow.

        I parked
on Route 4 by the graveyard,
wearing my new Christmas boots
that your brother's family gave me,
and hiked to your grave.
The snow was a foot deep, but stiff,
and I sank down only a little.
Gus danced and skittered, happy,
but not so happy as I was.

One day the temperature dropped
to zero, so icy I couldn't
walk Gus, and my knees hurt
like my mother's. Following

your advice, I took Advil.
I forgot to tell you: My tests
are good, no cancer, and my sugar
is stable. Sometimes for a week
I have trouble sleeping,
especially after a nightmare
when you leave me for someone else.

One weekend Andrew's family
stayed over for the night.
All three of the children
sat on my lap while I read stories
— and Emily liked my meatloaf.
Sometimes I read these letters aloud
to our friends.

            When you wrote
about lovemaking or cancer,
about absences or a quarrel,
I loved to turn up in your poems.
I imagined those you'd make
after I died; I regretted
I wouldn't be able to read them.

Although it's still light
at 5 P.M., the feeder goes unattended.
The woodpecker has done
with my suet for the day.
Red squirrels doze in their holes.
Chickadees sleep in the barn
or up hill in hemlock branches.

I want to sleep like the birds,
then wake to write you again
without hope that you read me.
If a car pulls into the drive
I want to hide in our bedroom
the way you hid sometimes
when people came calling.

Remembered happiness is agony;
so is remembered agony.
I live in a present compelled
by anniversaries and objects:
your pincushion; your white slipper;
your hooded Selectric II;
the label *basil* in a familiar hand;
a stain on flowery sheets.

LETTER AFTER A YEAR

Here's a story I never told you.
Living in a rented house
on South University in Ann Arbor
long before we met, I found
bundled letters in the attic room
where I took myself to work.
A young woman tenant of the attic
wrote these letters to her lover,
who had died in a plane crash.
In my thirtieth year, with tenure
and a new book coming out,
I read the letters in puzzlement.
"She's writing to somebody *dead?*"

There's one good thing
about April. Every day Gus and I
take a walk in the graveyard.
I'm the one who doesn't
piss on your stone. All winter
when ice and snow kept me away
I worried that you missed me.
"Perkins! Where the hell
are you?"

                In hell. Every day
I play in repertory the same
script without you, without love,
without audience except for Gus,
who waits attentive
for cues: a walk, a biscuit,
bedtime. The year of days

without you and your body swept by
as quick as an afternoon;
but each afternoon took a year.

At first in my outrage
I daydreamed burning the house:
kerosene in pie plates
with a candle lit in the middle.
I locked myself in your study
with Gus, Ada, and the rifle
my father gave me at twelve.
I killed our cat and our dog.
I swallowed a bottle of pills,
knowing that if I woke on fire
I had the gun.

        After you died
I stopped rereading history.
I took up Cormac McCarthy
for the rage and murder.
Now I return to Gibbon; secure
in his reasonable civilization,
he exercises detachment
as barbarians skewer Romans.
Then Huns gallop from the sunrise
wearing skulls.

        What's new?
I see more people now. In March,
I took Kate and Mary to Piero's.
At the end of the month ice dropped
to the pond's bottom, and water

flashed and flowed
through pines in western light.
The year melted into April
and I lived through the hour
we learned last year you would die.
For the next ten days, my mind
sat by our bed again
as you diminished cell by cell.

Last week the goldfinches
flew back for a second spring.
Again I witnessed snowdrops
worry from dead leaves
into air. Now your hillside
daffodils edge up, and today
it's a year since we set you down
at the border of the graveyard
on a breezy April day. We stood
in a circle around the coffin
and its hole, under pines
and birches, to lower you
into glacial sand.

When I dream
sometimes your hair is long
and we make love as we used to.
One nap time I saw your face
at eighty: many lines, more flesh,
the good bones distinct.

It's astonishing to be old.
When I stand after sitting,

I'm shocked at how I must stretch
to ease the stiffness out.
When we first spoke of marriage
we dismissed the notion
because you'd be a widow
twenty-five years, or maybe
I wouldn't be able to make love
while desire still flared in you.
Sometimes now I feel crazy
with desire again
as if I were forty, drinking,
and just divorced.

Ruth Houghton had a stroke.
Her daughter sent me the album
of photographs Roger took
in his documentary passion —
inside and outside our house,
every room, every corner —
one day in September 1984.
I howled as I gazed at that day
intact. Our furniture
looked out of place, as if vandals
had shoved everything awry.
There were pictures on the walls
we put away long ago.
The kitchen wallpaper shone
bright red in Roger's Kodacolor;
it faded as we watched
not seeing it fade.

WEEDS AND PEONIES

Your peonies burst out, white as snow squalls,
with red flecks at their shaggy centers
in your border of prodigies by the porch.
I carry one magnanimous blossom indoors
and float it in a glass bowl, as you used to do.

Ordinary pleasures, contentment recollected,
blow like snow into the abandoned garden,
overcoming the daisies. Your blue coat
vanishes down Pond Road into imagined snowflakes
with Gus at your side, his great tail swinging,

but you will not reappear, tired and satisfied,
and grief's repeated particles suffuse the air —
like the dog yipping through the entire night,
or the cat stretching awake, then curling
as if to dream of her mother's milky nipples.

A raccoon dislodged a geranium from its pot.
Flowers, roots, and dirt lay upended
in the back garden where lilies begin
their daily excursions above stone walls
in the season of old roses. I pace beside weeds

and snowy peonies, staring at Mount Kearsarge
where you climbed wearing purple hiking boots.
"Hurry back. Be careful, climbing down."
Your peonies lean their vast heads westward
as if they might topple. Some topple.

Library of Congress Cataloging-in-Publication Data

Hall, Donald, 1928–   .

Without / Donald Hall.

p.   cm.

ISBN 0-395-88408-X

ISBN 0-395-95765-6 (pbk.)

1. Elegiac poetry, American.   2. Hall, Donald, 1928–
— Marriage — Poetry.   3. Kenyon, Jane — Poetry.
4. Death — Poetry.   5. Grief — Poetry.

I. Title.

PS3515.A3152W58 1998

811'.54 — dc21   97-39925   CIP

A number of poems previously appeared, in earlier versions, in the follow-ing publications: *American Poetry Review*: Letter at Christmas. *Boston Book Review*: Her Long Illness. *DoubleTake*: Air Shatters in the Car's Small Room. *Georgia Review*: Last Days. *Gettysburg Review*: Midsummer Let-ter. *Harvard Review*: Letter from Washington. *Michigan Quarterly Review*: Letter in the New Year. *The New Criterion*: The Gallery; Independence Day Letter; Postcard: January 22nd. *The New York Times Magazine*: Weeds and Peonies. *The New Yorker*: The Porcelain Couple; The Ship Pounding. *Ontario Review*: Letter after a Year. *Ploughshares* vol. 22/4: Letter with No Address. *Poetry*: "A Beard for a Blue Pantry"; Midwinter Letter; With-out (also previously published in *The Old Life*, 1996). *Sewanee Review*: Blues for Polly; Song for Lucy. *Threepenny Review*: Letter in Autumn.